THE
GIFTED
AND
TALENTED

Gilda Berger

THE GIFTED AND TALENTED

FRANKLIN WATTS
NEW YORK | LONDON | TORONTO | SYDNEY | 1980
AN IMPACT BOOK

Diagrams by Vantage Art, Inc.

The California Short-Form Test of Mental Maturity reproduced on pages 27 and 28 by permission of the publisher, CTB/McGraw-Hill, Del Monte Research Park, Monterey, California 93940. Copyright © 1963, by McGraw-Hill, Inc. All rights reserved. Printed in the U.S.A. The tests on page 59 are adapted from the Torrance Tests of Creative Thinking, with permission of the publisher, Personnel Press, Inc. A division of Ginn and Company, Lexington, Mass.

Photographs courtesy of The New York Public Library Picture Collection: pp. 11, 14, 16, and 49; United Press International: p. 12; and the U.S. Department of the Interior, National Park Service, Edison National Historic Site: pp. 19 and 20.

Library of Congress Cataloging in Publication Data

Berger, Gilda.
The gifted and talented.

(An Impact book)
Includes bibliographies and index.
SUMMARY: Explains the terms "gifted" and "talented" and discusses the special needs of gifted individuals with emphasis on how these needs may be fulfilled by society, educational facilities, and the individuals themselves.
    1. Gifted children—Juvenile literature.
    [1. Gifted children] I. Title.
HQ773.5.B47   371.9′5   79-23967
ISBN 0-531-04111-5

Copyright © 1980 by Gilda Berger
All rights reserved
Printed in the United States of America
5 4 3 2 1

Contents

Chapter 1
INTRODUCTION
1

Chapter 2
WHAT IS GIFTEDNESS?
5

Chapter 3
HISTORY OF THE GIFTED
23

Chapter 4
THE GIFTED AT HOME
33

Chapter 5
THE GIFTED AT SCHOOL
39

Chapter 6
PROBLEMS OF THE GIFTED
45

Chapter 7
TESTING FOR GIFTEDNESS
53

Chapter 8
PROGRAMS FOR THE GIFTED
64

Chapter 9
THE DISADVANTAGED GIFTED
72

BIBLIOGRAPHY
81

FOR FURTHER READING
83

INDEX
85

THE GIFTED AND TALENTED

Chapter 1
INTRODUCTION

Do you know someone

> who always gets high marks in school?
> who has an outstanding memory?
> who quickly catches on to new ideas?
> who is curious and always eager to learn more?
> who is an outstanding dancer, actor, writer, artist?
> who is a leader among his or her friends?
> who comes up with imaginative, creative ideas?

> Is this person a friend?
> Someone in your class or school?
> A member of your family?
> Or is it you, yourself?

Such a person is called gifted or talented. Gifted or talented people show outstanding ability in one or more areas, including academic achievement, intellectual capacity, creative or productive thinking, leadership, or special talent in the performing or visual arts.

Among today's gifted and talented youngsters are tomorrow's outstanding figures, scientists such as Albert Einstein, inventors such as Thomas Edison, leaders such as John F. Kennedy, musicians such as Van Cliburn, writers such as Helen Keller, artists such as Pablo Picasso, dancers such as Martha Graham, and many, many others like them who will make important contributions to the world of the future.

According to the U.S. Office of Education, at least 3 percent of the 51 million children of school age in the United States—about 2 million American boys and girls—are gifted.

In a typical group of 100 students, for example, about 3 are gifted or talented. Of the others, about 68 are average, 13 are above average, 13 are below average, and 3 are retarded. Among the three children who are gifted, there is one who is considered highly gifted. Among every one million youngsters, there is one so highly gifted that he or she is called a genius.

The gifted are found everywhere—in cities and suburbs and on farms all across the country. They are girls and boys, black and white, rich and poor, Christians and Jews, from long-standing as well as culturally different American families.

Some of these gifted and talented youngsters receive educational opportunities to develop their special abilities. They become musicians and mathematicians, poets and philosophers, scientists and senators.

But many others never get the special help they need to develop fully. Through lack of attention or lack of opportunities, these youngsters either hide their abilities or do not accomplish all that is possible for them.

Gifted children are a valuable national resource. Yet for many years people have said, "The gifted are smart enough to learn without extra help." Or, "In a democracy, what is good for everyone is good enough for the gifted." As a result, the gifted rarely receive the special services they need, and this much-needed resource is being wasted.

In 1972 the U.S. Office of the Gifted and Talented reported that only 4 percent, or about 80,000 gifted students, were receiving the special educational services they needed. In 1977 that number had increased to about 12 percent. The picture surely has brightened. Yet the overwhelming majority still does not receive any special attention.

Research shows that many gifted students do not succeed on their own. Without special assistance, many gifted youngsters get turned off by school. They become disruptive or have frequent absences. Some drop out of high school before graduation. And many others achieve only average or below-average marks in school.

In March 1972, a report was made to Congress by U.S. Commissioner of Education Sidney P. Marland, which contained three main points:

1. Even though most people do not realize it, gifted children are often ignored or neglected in the classroom.
2. The full development of the minds and abilities of the young is an important function of government.
3. In order to grow and prosper, society needs the intellectual and creative contributions of its most gifted children.

Where special programs are offered, gifted and talented students benefit. They achieve more as children, and more often become successful adults. They are less likely to feel superior or inferior to the people around them.

More and more people are coming to realize that youngsters with outstanding abilities are a minority in society that needs the same considerations as other minorities. Special education provisions are required the same as for children who are retarded or disadvantaged socially or economically. In a democracy every child should have an equal opportunity to develop to the greatest extent possible.

All children can benefit from learning that, while they are alike in most ways, they are different in some ways. They can come to understand that even though they are members of a general population, they also hold a special place in the world. By learning who they are, and what they can do, the gifted and talented, like all other children, can help not only themselves, but also the society in which they live.

Chapter 2
WHAT IS GIFTEDNESS?

Kathy is the top student in her sixth-grade class. She gets the highest marks on tests and the best grades on report cards. She is the first one to grasp new ideas, to learn new facts, and to develop new skills—from learning to use a slide rule to staining glass. Sometimes the teacher asks Kathy to explain hard-to-understand material to others in her class, since she almost always finishes her work ahead of everyone else.

When Kathy works on her own, she shows two special traits. One is that she often finds new and original ways to solve problems, rather than using the standard approach. And the other is that she sticks to the project until she succeeds. She does not give up easily.

Kathy is the first violinist in the school orchestra and sings soprano in the school chorus. At home she takes piano lessons and plays jazz as well as classical music. When her teacher needs a sign or poster made, he asks Kathy to prepare it because of her skill in drawing and lettering. For the past two years Kathy has been given the leading role in the class play.

Kathy is tall and very attractive. She studies ballet and gymnastics. She has already appeared in children's roles with the local professional ballet company. Her gymnastics teacher has entered her in several statewide competitions, where she won either gold or silver medals.

One of Kathy's hobbies is magic. She has been paid to perform at children's birthday parties in the neighborhood. Another hobby is ham radio operating. Kathy speaks to people all over the United States on her ham set and knows many other hams by name. Airplanes have always fascinated her. She can easily describe the engines, speed, cost, capacity, and other details of planes flown by the airlines.

Along with these special abilities and interests is Kathy's popularity. She is well liked by both boys and girls her age as well as by adults. She is a natural leader. Her friends turn to her for advice, ask her for suggestions, and generally follow her direction. Still, she is very thoughtful and considerate and is careful not to hurt anyone's feelings.

Kathy, however, is not a real person. She is a composite figure, one who displays nearly all the traits and characteristics of giftedness. No one gifted child has all of these qualities. The typical gifted and talented child, however, has many or even most of them.

Gifted children usually show a range of abilities. They are outstanding in some areas, average in others. Some get exceptionally high marks in their academic work, others are better at creative learning, while still others excel in the arts. While it is rare to find a gifted youngster who is superior in every area, as a group the gifted are above average in almost all areas and superior in many of them. In general, they show remarkable achievement and unusual ability for their age.

Giftedness is very complex. It has many sides. It takes many forms. It changes and grows from birth until death. It is just one part of a person's total development. Yet it is related to all other areas of growth.

Many people, over the years, have worked to prepare a good definition of giftedness. These definitions vary considerably.

At one extreme there are those who define giftedness only by superior intellectual or mental ability. According to these definitions, anyone with an IQ over a certain number, usually 120, is gifted. A child with an IQ over 180 is considered to be a genius.

Generally speaking, IQ, or intelligence quotient, is arrived at by comparing a child's mental age with his or her chronological age and multiplying by 100. This is usually presented as $IQ = \frac{\text{mental age}}{\text{chronological age}} \times 100$.

Mental age is determined by a child's performance on certain standardized tests. A ten-year-old child who scores the same as the average ten-year-old would have an IQ of 100 ($IQ = \frac{10}{10} \times 100$). If a ten-year-old performs like an average twelve-year-old on the test, then the IQ would be 120 ($IQ = \frac{12}{10} \times 100$).

The problem here is that many gifted people do not do well on IQ tests. For one reason or another, some youngsters with many characteristics of giftedness do poorly in testing situations. Thus, many aspects of intelligence are not measured by the popular tests of intellectual ability. In fact, some educators say that the only thing that intelligence tests measure is the ability to take intelligence tests.

At the other extreme are those who define gifted-

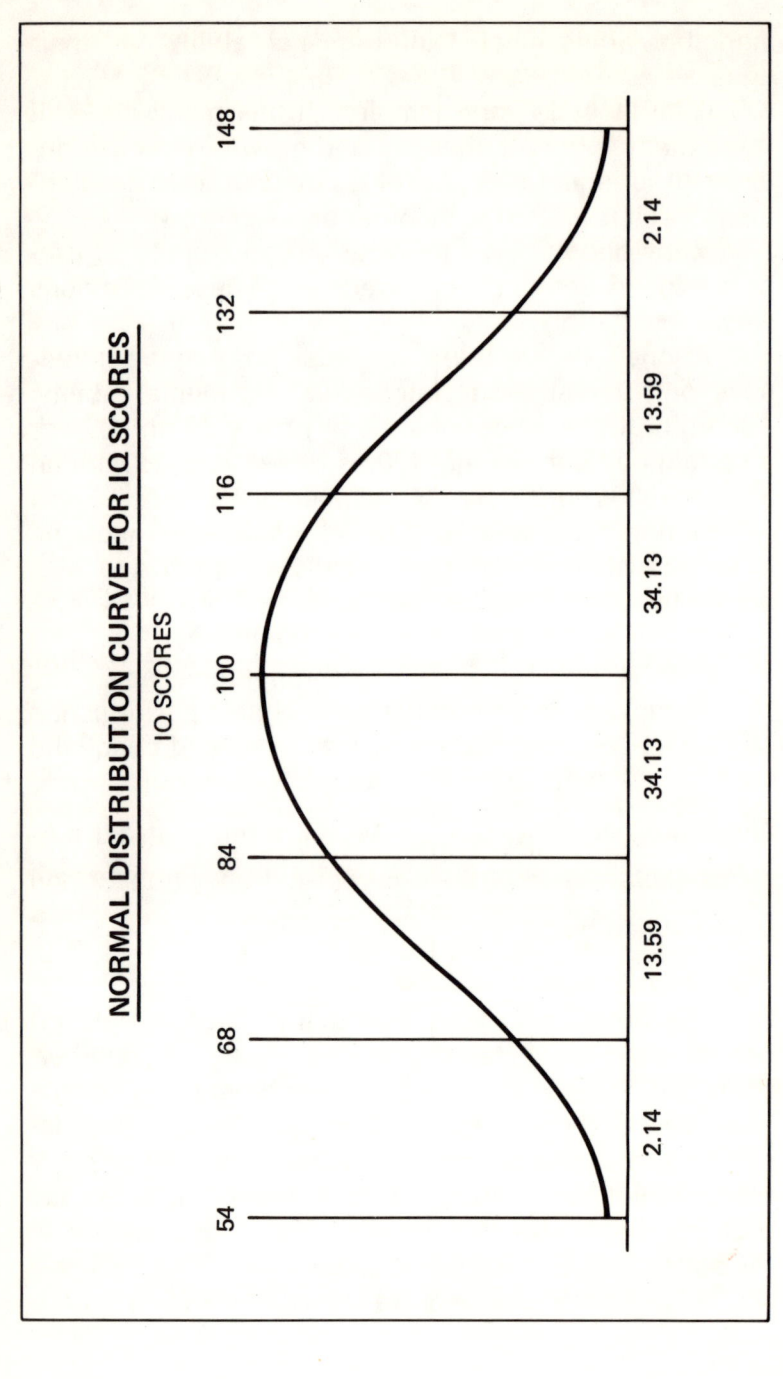

ness as either the proven ability or future potential to do remarkably well in some valuable human activity.

However, this type of definition suffers from being too vague. How well do you have to perform to be considered "remarkable"? What human activities are "valuable"? And who is to judge "proven ability," or "future potential"?

One definition now widely accepted was given by the U.S. Office of Education: Children who are capable of high performance include those with demonstrated achievement and/or potential ability in one or more of these areas: 1. general intellectual ability; 2. specific academic areas; 3. creative or productive thinking; 4. leadership; 5. visual or performing arts aptitude; and 6. the culturally different gifted.

Many people agree with Joseph S. Renzulli's conclusions drawn from his own research on the gifted. According to Renzulli, a gifted person has three sets of traits: 1. above-average intellectual ability; 2. creativity; and 3. the motivation and drive to stick to a task.

Perhaps the simplest definition is one that sums up the others: A gifted child is one who does things a little earlier, a little faster, a little better, and a little differently. This definition is useful for taking a closer look at the development of the qualities of giftedness.

"A LITTLE EARLIER"

Gifted and talented children go through the same developmental stages as all children. But one of the first signs of giftedness may be early physical development.

Average children sit up at seven months. The child who is gifted may sit up at five or six months of age. Average children walk by fifteen months. Many gifted children walk before they are one year old.

The gifted child usually starts to talk at an early age, using an advanced vocabulary. The average two-year-old might say, "I see a bird." A gifted two-year-old might say, "I see a bird in the tree. It has a worm in its beak. The bird is going to eat the worm."

Most gifted children also show signs of curiosity and persistence early in life. Typical four-year-olds may just burst into tears when told that mother will be late coming home. Gifted four-year-olds might ask questions like, "Where is she?" "Why will she be late?" "How is she traveling?" "Who is with her?" "What time will she be back?" And they will keep asking questions until they are satisfied with the answers.

By the age of three, many of the gifted can count to one thousand as well as recognize and write all the letters of the alphabet. By the time they are four, 60 percent of the gifted are able to read. Many are self taught. Benjamin Franklin started to read at such an early age that he had no memory of ever learning how.

Very young children who are gifted are often able to concentrate for long periods of time without being distracted. Many gifted one-year-olds are able to listen to a story for ten minutes, or even longer. They often listen in on stories that are being read to older brothers or sisters.

Some gifted children show unusual insight for their age. Albert Einstein, for instance, was stirred by the sight of a compass at the age of five. He later recalled his feeling, that for the first time he became

**Albert Einstein,
at about age six.
His sister Maja is
standing beside him.**

aware that "something deeply hidden had to be behind things."

"A LITTLE FASTER"

The gifted child learns quickly and easily. He or she usually requires fewer explanations and less repetition than most other children. That is why many gifted children become impatient in school with meaningless drills or "busywork" assignments.

Many have a quick memory for factual information. One four-year-old, who was able to remember difficult terms after having heard them only once, was interested in dinosaurs. Words such as *brontosaurus* and *tyrannosaurus* quickly became part of his everyday vocabulary.

Also, gifted children are able to grasp abstract ideas very quickly. Karl Friedrich Gauss was one of the greatest mathematicians of all time. At the age of ten, when asked to find the sum of all numbers from one to one hundred, he hit on a formula to find the sum in a moment. Between the ages of fourteen and seventeen he made many of the fundamental discoveries that are the basis of modern mathematics.

Surely one of the most amazing examples of early giftedness was Christian Heinrich Heinecken. Heinecken was born in Germany in 1721. By the age of ten months, he was able to speak. By one year, he could retell many of the stories in the Bible. By the age of two, he was an expert in Biblical history, and by three he was able to speak German, French, and Latin. At four years of age, Heinecken began to study com-

Einstein's discoveries in the field of physics forever marked him as a true genius.

parative religion and church history. He also learned to write. His achievements became so well known that scholars came to visit with him. Unfortunately, Heinecken died of unknown causes at the age of four-and-one-half.

Lorin Maazel, the world-famous orchestra conductor, showed as a child the traits necessary to a successful career in music—love of music, perfect pitch, and an excellent musical memory. By the age of ten, Maazel had already conducted in New York's Carnegie Hall. He then conducted throughout Europe and America before attaining his high position as Music Director of the Cleveland Orchestra while still a young man.

Many scientists make their most significant discoveries while still in their twenties. Some famous artists created outstanding paintings while still in their teens.

"A LITTLE BETTER"

For years people held a standard picture of a gifted child in mind. The child was physically small and weak, ailing, and almost always wearing glasses. In addition, he or she was anxious and nervous, self-centered, and difficult to get along with.

The 1959 report by Lewis Terman of 1,500 gifted people went a long way to disproving this image. The study, which was conducted over a twenty-five-year period, showed that, on the contrary, members of this group are generally physically attractive and superior to others in size, strength, and general health.

Christian Heinrich Heinecken lived to be only four-and-a-half-years old but was already world famous for his genius.

As a group, they are well adjusted socially and get along better than average with their parents and friends. They usually exhibit fewer emotional problems than other people. Further, they tend to be more independent, more confident, and more mature psychologically than others of the same age and sex.

In 1962 Victor and Mildred Goertzel published a study of famous individuals of high achievement in many fields. They reported that the group had extraordinary leadership abilities, common sense, and keen powers of observation and perseverance.

Recent research has added even more traits common to the gifted and talented. These include greater alertness, a better sense of humor, and higher expectations for success.

"A LITTLE DIFFERENTLY"

Besides developing earlier and faster, the gifted show certain abilities most average children never display. In addition to their ability to think abstractly, for example, they show a greater awareness of their surroundings, a drive to master new and difficult ideas, and an ability to learn by themselves.

John Milton, the great English poet, was already familiar with Greek and Hebrew, as well as English, by age twelve. He said that he read the classics in all three languages until midnight every night.

Blaise Pascal, the seventeenth century French scholar, was taught only Greek and Latin as a child. Yet he was able, on his own, to work out most of the basic laws of geometry by the age of eleven.

Lorin Maazel at nine was already an accomplished orchestra conductor.

Gifted youngsters have a way of thinking that organizes and relates their experiences. One gifted six-year-old, after watching a TV program on poverty, connected separate bits of information that she had acquired and told her parents that she now understood how poverty and illness were related.

Gifted and talented children show broad and ever-changing patterns of interest. These interests may include science and math and games requiring abstract thinking skills. Thomas Alva Edison began doing scientific experiments at the age of nine to test the statements in a chemistry book that his mother gave him. Roger T. Peterson, the famed naturalist, developed a lifelong interest in birds beginning at age five.

Many gifted children are avid collectors. One kindergartner collected leaves from twenty-two trees of various kinds. She pasted them in a book, printed their names below, and took them to school for Show and Tell. She then explained what made leaves change color.

The gifted have been shown to be more concerned with moral and social issues than is usual. They have a particular interest in the realities of life and death. Often they are more introspective and sensitive.

Many gifted are highly imaginative too. One three-year-old, after seeing her first ballet performance, decided to become a ballerina. She spent hours on her own creating dance steps to the music of Tchaikovsky and others.

Thomas Alva Edison showed many early signs of giftedness. Here he is seen as a boy and (over) as a young man sitting in front of one of his most famous inventions, the tinfoil phonograph.

The creatively gifted are often able to come up with imaginative solutions to difficult problems. They think independently and not always along traditional paths. Along with this is often a feeling of playfulness combined with a strong urge to stick to a task until it is completed. One study of top-rated entering college freshmen showed gifted children to be less authoritarian and less rigid than average. They are people who tend to take chances in the world of ideas.

Those who are gifted creators get most of their ideas from within rather than by imitation or through instruction. Ludwig van Beethoven, one of the greatest composers of all time, studied musical composition with leading composers such as Mozart and Haydn. But he borrowed little of their writing style. Instead, he went his own way, creating completely new and original works. Of his approach, Beethoven once said: "You will ask me where I get my ideas. They come unsummoned—in the open air, in the woods, at dawn."

Giftedness, then, has many aspects, takes many forms, and evolves in particular ways in different individuals. There is no single key to unlock the many complexities of giftedness.

Yet the simple checklist below can give you a rough idea of your own giftedness. All "yes" answers do not necessarily mean that you are gifted and talented, just as all "no" answers do not mean that you are not. But if you answer "yes" to most questions, it is fair to say you have many traits and characteristics of giftedness.

CHECKLIST FOR STUDENTS

1. Did you walk and talk earlier than most children?
2. Did you always get good grades in school?
3. Did you show an early interest in books?

4. Have you an extensive vocabulary for your age?
5. Are you curious about how things work and where they come from?
6. Have you a wide range of interests or hobbies?
7. Have you a good memory?
8. Have you a long attention span?
9. Do you like to do things on your own?
10. Do you enjoy solving difficult problems?
11. Can you figure out new and original ways to accomplish tasks?
12. Can you relate new knowledge to what you already know?
13. Do you perceive abstract ideas rapidly?
14. Does your writing, drawing, or dancing often include original and imaginative ideas?
15. Do you prefer the company of older and brighter people?
16. Do you get along very well with most youngsters your own age?
17. Do your friends look to you as a leader?
18. Are you sensitive to the needs and feelings of others?
19. Do you show an interest in social problems?
20. Have you a very good sense of humor?

Chapter 3
HISTORY OF THE GIFTED

HISTORICAL ROOTS

In primitive times, it was believed that unusual strength, knowledge, or other special abilities were divine gifts. The very bright and very talented were often given special positions in the tribe. They became the tribal leaders or the medicine men.

At the same time, though, exceptional abilities were thought to be somehow connected with madness. Creativity was linked to emotional disturbance or insanity. Some people even regarded mental strength as a sign of physical disease.

The first attempt we know of to identify the gifted occurred in China around the year 2200 B.C. A person wishing to apply for a government position had to take a competitive examination. The exam was designed to identify the most gifted and able persons from amongst all who sought the post.

From the Bible we learn that a small number of the gifted became the priests and judges of their tribes. This was because they were believed to be the wisest and the most knowing. In Chapter 17 of the *Book of Deuteronomy,* the people are ordered to bring their questions and disputes before the priests and the judges.

In his great work *The Republic*, the ancient Greek philosopher Plato said that in his ideal state, only the most brilliant would rule. To find leaders, youths who showed great promise at an early age would be carefully watched. They would be given tasks with instructions difficult to remember or easy to confuse. Then, "He who remembers and is not deceived is to be elected."

According to Plato the highest ruler, the philosopher-king, would be intellectually eager and able to learn easily; be steady, brave, and good-looking; have a strong sense of morality and toughness; and have the aptitude to be trained and developed in these directions.

The Middle Ages were bad times for people of curiosity and imagination. The powerful Church taught that there were many questions that should not be asked.

One of the first steps in educating the gifted, however, came during this period. Emperor Charlemagne, around the year A.D. 800, decreed that the state would educate the outstanding children of the common people, instead of just the children of the rich and high-born.

The fifteenth and sixteenth centuries, known as the Renaissance, were a time of tremendous growth in learning in the arts and in the sciences. The human mind was freed of many of the restraints of the past.

Gifted Renaissance people accomplished amazing things in many different fields. Among the outstanding figures of the Renaissance were writers such as Shakespeare, Cervantes, and Petrarch; artists such as Michelangelo, Leonardo da Vinci, and Raphael; scientists such as Copernicus and Galileo; explorers such as Columbus and Magellan; and thinkers such as Erasmus and Luther. They all flourished under the very favorable conditions of those times.

During the middle years of the Renaissance, the sultan Mohammed the Conqueror greatly advanced learning and the arts in Turkey and the Mideast by building a famous boys' school, the Court of the Eight Colleges, within the mosque in Constantinople.

Only the most intelligent, strongest, and best-looking boys were admitted to the school. They were selected from the lands Mohammed had conquered, without regard to social class. The goal of the school was to create "fine minds in hardened bodies."

The graduates of the school took posts in either the civil or the military service of the government. The success of the Turkish Empire during this period was probably due to the education these gifted young men received in the sultan's palace school.

AMERICAN EDUCATION

In the early years of the United States, Thomas Jefferson put forth a bill for the "Diffusion of Education." Influenced by Plato's *Republic,* Jefferson proposed that promising youths be educated in universities at public expense. They would receive training in the arts and sciences in order to eventually fill key positions of leadership in the new country.

Difficult, competitive tests were set up. Jefferson's hope was that "the best geniuses will be raked from the rubbish annually, and sent to William and Mary College. By this means we hope to avail the State of those talents which nature has sown as liberally among the poor as the rich, but which perish without use, if not sought for and cultivated."

One of the first special programs in the education of the gifted ran from 1868 to the end of the nineteenth century in the schools of St. Louis, Missouri. This program allowed the gifted to skip grades in what was called flexible promotion. High-achieving students could complete the six years of grammar school in four years.

Between 1900 and 1926 many school districts set up special programs for the gifted. These included flexible promotion, special classes, and special schools for high academic achievers. The object was usually to accelerate, or speed up, the education of gifted learners. Children of high intelligence, it was argued, should be educated separately so that they would not be held back by the slower learners. The goal was to prepare the gifted for positions of leadership.

The term *gifted child* came into popular use during this period. However, it referred to the child with outstanding intellectual ability only. The main tool used to identify the gifted was IQ score, which was based either on standardized group intelligence tests, such as the California Tests of Mental Maturity, or individual IQ tests, such as the Wechsler Intelligence Scale for Children (WISC) or the Stanford-Binet Intelligence Scale.

During this same period one of the most amazing child prodigies came to worldwide attention. At the age of nine, William James Sidis passed the entrance exam for Harvard University. Though the university made him wait two years, he entered in 1909 at the age of eleven.

From then on, though, nothing went right for Sidis. He never accomplished anything of distinction. He died alone when he was only forty-six years of age.

The great publicity given to Sidis's failure proved to be very bad for the gifted around the country. Many plans to accelerate the gifted or to place them

Here and over: Sample selections from the California Tests of Mental Maturity.

TEST 1

DIRECTIONS: In each row there is one picture that shows something which is the opposite of the first picture. Find it and mark its number.

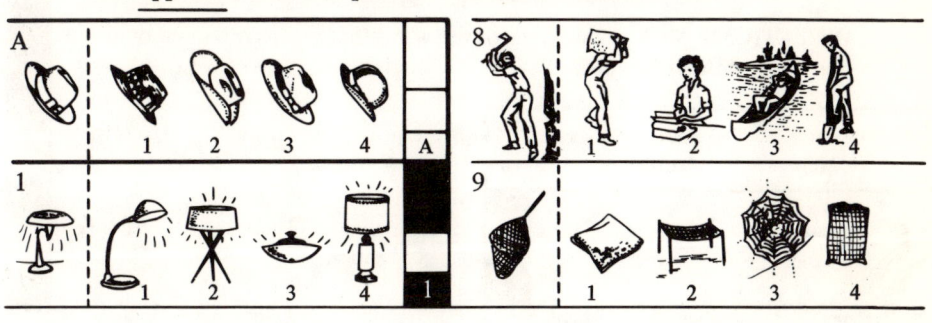

TEST 4

DIRECTIONS: Mark the letter L for each picture that shows a left and the letter R for each picture that shows a right.

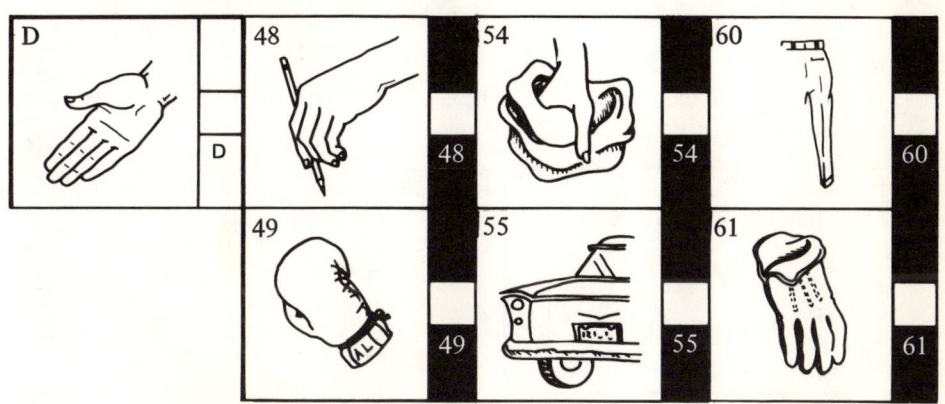

TEST 6

DIRECTIONS: Mark the number of the word that means the same or about the same as the first word.

F. blossom	¹ tree	² vine
	³ flower	⁴ garden

71. conceal   ¹ pitch   ² hide
         ³ color   ⁴ corner

72. tone   ¹ wild   ² book
         ³ reveal   ⁴ pitch

83. expose   ¹ relate   ² construct
         ³ disclose   ⁴ decant

84. winsome   ¹ chary   ² charming
         ³ critical   ⁴ valid

85. tumult   ¹ illness   ² infamy
         ³ commotion   ⁴ gait

TEST 8

DIRECTIONS: Work these problems. Use scratch paper if necessary. Mark the letter of each correct answer.

K. If you earned $5.00 and spent $3.00, how many dollars would you have left?
   a $1.00
   b $2.00
   c $3.00
   d $5.00

145. There are 20 girls in the Sunday school class. Every week each girl gives 5¢ to go toward a fund for needy families. How much will all the girls give in 5 weeks?
   a $1.00
   b 25¢
   c $5.00
   d $7.50

in special classes or schools were dropped. Once more, the gifted were thought to be slightly strange, and special education was suspected of having harmful effects.

Research on the gifted continued nevertheless. In 1926, Dr. Harvey Zorbaugh set up a clinic for the study of the gifted at New York University in New York City. His interest grew out of his meeting with a young safecracker in 1924. The criminal, he found, had an amazing IQ of 168. Where had he learned so much about the explosives he had used in his robberies? By reading books in the public library! Stanford University in California also established research projects dealing with the gifted.

Lewis Terman's research findings on 1,500 California children with IQs over 140 helped to overthrow the notion that giftedness is linked to strange behavior or madness. His studies, and Catherine Cox's study of great men of the past, showed that the gifted differ from the average only in degree, rather than in kind. Most of those in the highest 10 percent of mental ability, they found, possessed superior physical, social, moral, and emotional traits as well. Also, they decided, IQ was a good predictor of adult achievement.

During the 1930s and 1940s, when Progressive Education was in favor, special classes for the gifted gave way to enrichment programs that were taught in the regular classroom. Instead of going faster, the gifted were taught at the same speed as everyone else. But they were encouraged to learn the subjects in greater detail and to explore related material.

Leta Hollingsworth, in 1942, was one of the first researchers to bring to light some of the problems of the gifted. She studied the effects of special programs on their social and scholastic development and uncovered some underlying social and academic problems of gifted youngsters both in and out of the special programs.

But the most dramatic change in the education of the gifted occurred in 1957 as a result of the Russian launch of *Sputnik,* the first shot into outer space. Americans were shocked to find out that other countries, such as the Soviet Union, were doing more than the United States to train and use their best minds.

Suddenly U.S. educators got the go-ahead to expand and improve educational programs to meet the needs of the nation. The federal government encouraged the states to provide special programs for gifted and talented children. The result was a strong emphasis on the discovery and training of scientific talent. Along with this, the focus of the gifted programs shifted from children nine to twelve years old to youngsters of high school and college age.

In 1958 the National Defense Education Act was passed. This law mostly helped children with special abilities in math and science. Many felt it was designed to help the United States catch up with the Soviet Union rather than further the education of all the gifted.

In the early 1960s there was a shift away from using only IQ scores to identify giftedness. Most of the new ideas came from J. P. Guilford's analysis of the human intellect. Guilford identified 150 areas of intelligence, of which IQ tests measure twenty-four at the most. The IQ, he pointed out, does not pay attention to such important traits as character, personality, perseverance in tasks, or creativity.

Now "broad band" methods of identification began to be used. These considered creativity, independence, leadership, and other personality traits, along with IQ scores and achievement test results. During the 1960s, too, there was the beginning of interest in finding "hidden" giftedness, especially among poor and minority youth.

E. Paul Torrance and others studied the differences between the highly intelligent and those identified as highly creative. What they found was very surprising. Highly creative children achieved the same level of success as highly intelligent children, even though their IQs were an average of 23 points lower. If intelligence tests alone were used to identify the gifted, they would miss 70 percent of the highly creative.

Despite the boom in education in the 1960s, the gifted received little extra help or funding. Late in 1969, however, Senator Jacob Javits called for a study on how to meet the needs of the gifted. The report that came out showed a serious lack of educational services for the gifted. Only ten states had any programs at all. There was a clear need for federal support.

In 1972 Congress created the Office of the Gifted and Talented within the Office of Education. Two years later they funded Section 404 of Public Law 93-380, known as the Special Projects Act, which provided $2.5 million every year to state and local agencies for various special educational projects. This averaged out to about $1 per year for each gifted and talented child in the nation.

On November 2, 1978, President Jimmy Carter signed Public Law 95-561. This bill, known as the Education Amendments of 1978, authorizes funds through 1983 for elementary and secondary education programs. Title IX-A of this bill is the Gifted and Talented Act. It promises increasing amounts of monies to state education agencies to help them plan, develop, and improve programs designed to help gifted and talented children. It makes special provision for disadvantaged gifted and talented youth. And it provides grants for training people to work with gifted and talented children in many kinds of programs.

This act is a great step forward. It is sparking the public's awareness of the needs of the gifted. It is encouraging organizations to work even harder to promote both the study and the education of the gifted and talented. And it is backing up with money our belief that every human being is a unique individual with an equal right to the full development of his or her potential.

The history of the gifted shows an increasing recognition of the rights, the needs, and the value of the gifted and talented person in our society. It reflects some profound changes in our understanding of intelligence and the functioning of the human mind. It is full of promise for the days to come.

Chapter 4
THE GIFTED AT HOME

Not every child who is interested in science can become a great scientist like Marie Curie. Not every child who likes to paint can become a great artist like Marc Chagall. What each child achieves is limited by the ability with which he or she is born.

But even a very high inborn capacity does not guarantee great achievement. Achievement also depends on the experiences that come after birth. While some gifted and talented children do survive in spite of adverse conditions, outstanding ability needs to be recognized early, encouraged, and helped to grow. The leader of the civil rights movement Martin Luther King, Jr., the fine writer Pearl S. Buck, and the brilliant violinist Isaac Stern all succeeded because they were born with high ability *and* because their abilities were nurtured with love and attention.

From contact with parents or other adults, infants begin to get a self-concept, a feeling of who they are. Children who have a great deal of close physical contact with loving adults are more likely to develop a positive self-concept. They feel valued and secure. Research shows a close connection between positive self-concept and success in school.

The talents of George and Ira Gershwin, one a composer the other a lyric writer, were fostered in their home. It was a happy, busy household where everyone worked hard. The parents hoped for and expected things of their children. The children were treated with respect and were listened to. They knew that their parents cared what happened to them.

Other family members can also provide stimulation for very young children. Grandparents, cousins, aunts, and uncles can increase the youngsters' awareness of the world by pointing out sights and smells. The well-known scientist Cornelia Downs once said, "Grandmother spent hours in the garden with me developing my 'seeing eye.' From her I discovered that half of learning to be a scientist lies in having your eyes opened to the world of nature."

Parents who allow their gifted children to act like children, and who provide them with both stimulation and the freedom to explore, make it possible for their children to develop their gifts to the fullest. Gifted children need to do all the things that are part of a normal, happy childhood. They need to watch TV and play with other children. They need help in mastering such skills as bike riding and rope jumping.

Gifted children often ask many, many questions. They are very curious about most things. One mother of a three-year-old said, "She wears me out with her questions. And she won't give up easily, either." Parents should recognize the value of this curiosity. They should answer their children's questions truthfully. They should guide them in asking good questions, and in making good guesses at the answers.

Parents can also help their children find information to satisfy their curiosity. Helping them gather information from encyclopedias, dictionaries, and other reference books is very important. Looking things up and sharing information helps children develop independent learning skills.

Most of the gifted show an early interest in books. Parents should read to them. In discussing the stories, in talking about the characters, actions, ideas, and meanings, adults can help understandings to grow. Young children who are able to read should have attractive books at home that are of interest to them and are on their own reading level.

When parents read a lot themselves, children usually want to read, too. Also, if parents attend lectures, the theater, museums, and concerts, children grow up thinking of these activities as fun and of interest. When TV programs are shared, they become even more meaningful for the children.

Children frequently grow up valuing the same kinds of achievement as their parents. Children who have parents that admire great writers, thinkers, and actors will do the same. When taught to value social contributions of others, they also become socially aware, and eventually may use their giftedness for the good of society.

Being part of the parents' world can be a very valuable experience for gifted and talented children. George M. Cohan, famous actor, playwright, and composer, was born into a theatrical family. He was carried on stage as a baby in a skit written by his father. His acting ability developed so fast that he made his debut in a professional stage production at the age of nine.

Young gifted children can be helped to develop interests and hobbies. Some of the toys parents buy should be ones that develop physical and mental abilities. The best toys require manual dexterity and the use of problem-solving or decision-making skills. As children grow older, they should have materials, space, and time to work at activities that are challenging.

William Clench, the zoologist, was encouraged in his collecting hobbies as a very young child. When he was a first-grader he built up a collection of salamanders and tadpoles while on a summer vacation in New York's Catskill Mountains. His parents encouraged his interest and even helped him move his collection to their Brooklyn home at the end of the summer.

Dr. Edward C. Kendall, Nobel prizewinner in science, constructed doorbells, telegraphs, and a lathe from found materials as a child. When his son, Hugh, a physicist, was growing up, Dr. Kendall and his wife let the boy hold movie shows in their home for fifty to one hundred children with equipment he had made by himself.

Travel stimulates ideas and the development of certain abilities. Children can help plan the trip and thus learn a great deal about the region they will be visiting. They can be taught how to read maps and how to figure mileage. Zoos, art galleries, museums, and factories can be visited, photographed, and talked about later. While traveling, there are also opportunities to play number, spelling, or memory games that can improve skills.

Parents should encourage their children to daydream and have fantasies. Role-playing, acting out stories, reading and writing fantastic tales, painting, sculpting, drawing—all can be important to a child's growth. If these types of activities are fostered in young children, they may result in original and creative thinking later on.

There is little question that childhood experiences at home affect development. Research has found that gifted children of about equal ability when young show wide differences in achievement as they grow up. Family background influences children's habits, interests, personality, and lifelong goals.

In their 1962 book *Cradles Of Eminence,* Victor and Mildred Goertzel reported on 400 outstanding world figures of the twentieth century. They found that the parents of these gifted individuals did much more than feed and clothe their children. They taught them faith in themselves, love of learning, and concern for social and moral issues, among other values.

Most of these figures had good opinions of themselves as young people. They read a great deal. They experienced more, traveled more, had more hobbies, and in general did more things on their own than most others of their age. They had close ties with intelligent adults. Above all, there was a strong drive to succeed in both the parents and the children.

Since parents have such a big impact on their children's learning skills and abilities, they should stay involved in the education process as their children go through school. The development of giftedness is an ongoing concern. Parents need to be partners with teachers and school officials in developing their children's potential.

If you think you are gifted, study the checklist below and discuss it with your family. If you can answer "yes" to most or all of the questions, then you truly have "gifted" parents—parents who encourage your giftedness.

PARENT CHECKLIST

1. Do your parents encourage you to explore, ask questions, and try to find answers?
2. Do they answer your questions honestly, patiently, and good-naturedly?
3. Do they help you to develop physical and social skills, as well as mental abilities?
4. Do they help you learn how to get along with others?

5. Do they guide you in making your own plans and decisions?
6. Do they help you find worthwhile and challenging materials to read and TV programs to watch?
7. Do you have plenty of books, including reference books, in your home library?
8. Are you provided with hobby materials and other things that are good for developing imagination and skills?
9. Do your parents regard fantasy as healthy and encourage you to make up stories and play-act?
10. Are you provided with a place to work at your hobbies?
11. Are you taken on trips to zoos, museums, historical sites, and other points of interest?
12. Do your parents help you generalize from your experiences and show you how to apply what you learn?
13. Do your parents encourage you to share in their hobbies and interests?
14. Do they show interest in your schoolwork and in how well you are doing in school?

Chapter 5
THE GIFTED AT SCHOOL

A number of gifted children were asked what they look for in a teacher. Among their answers were these:

"One who doesn't expect you to be right always."
"One who doesn't restrict your imagination."
"One who has a sense of humor."
"One who encourages you to work alone, but is there when you need help."
"One who laughs when something is not funny but you want it to be."

These comments point up some important ways that teachers help highly intelligent and talented children to learn and grow. Gifted youngsters, especially, need encouragement and aid in fitting into the educational system.

In all successful classrooms the teacher is aware of each child's unique abilities. The teacher respects each child's own learning pattern and tries to provide the most appropriate instruction and best experiences.

Providing for the gifted is a natural extension of this idea. The teacher of gifted and talented students involves the students in activities appropriate for them out of respect for their special ways of learning.

Good teachers do more than teach the basic skills. They train the gifted children in higher levels of thinking. They help the children learn to ask better questions. They provide them with opportunities to apply an inquiry approach to their studies. They prepare them to work independently.

Thinking and learning are very closely related. Two children given the problem of dividing four by two may arrive at the same answer. But one may get the answer by rote memory and one by a problem-solving process. Intellectual development begins with types of learning that require simple processes and proceeds to those that are increasingly complex.

Benjamin S. Bloom's taxonomy of thinking skills is one of the more popular models that teachers use to meet the specific needs of gifted students. In this approach, the teacher provides special materials that relate to the specific levels of the child's thinking skills. These levels, or stages, range from simple recall to creative synthesizing.

One way of teaching a more complex thinking skill is illustrated by this question: "What day follows the day before yesterday if two days from now will be Sunday?"

The kind of thinking through analysis that is needed to find the answer to this question can be taught this way: If two days from now will be Sunday, then one day from now will be Saturday, and so today must be Friday. If today is Friday, then yesterday was Thursday, the day before yesterday was Wednesday, and the day that follows Wednesday is Thursday. The correct answer, therefore, is Thursday.

While teachers of the gifted and talented are aware of their charges' unique abilities, they also understand that the children *are* children. They do not expect a child who is performing at a higher than average mental age to be necessarily as advanced in his or her emotional behavior.

The teacher who has a good self-concept can help gifted children to understand themselves. With a little help the children can learn to cope with social rejection or other problems that may come as a result of their high level of functioning.

Creative children often misbehave in school. They resist direction, show dislike for routine and drills, and are critical of others. After six months at a rigid high school in Munich, Germany, a teacher called Albert Einstein into an office and told him that it would be best if he left the school. "Your mere presence," said the teacher, "spoils the respect of the class for me."

Since gifted children, in particular, raise all kinds of questions, educators of these children need to accept and encourage this sign of giftedness. They should inspire children to think along unconventional lines, to express their own ideas, and to think things through for themselves. They should let them try out creative solutions to problems. And they should help them feel comfortable about making mistakes or trying out wild ideas that may not work out.

During one math lesson, a fourth-grader said she had a better rule for solving problems than the one the teacher was reading. "So! You think you know more than the book," the teacher fumed. "No," the child replied, "I don't think I know more than the book. But I like my rule better." The teacher glared at the student and went on with the lesson.

Another teacher faced with a similar situation let the child tell about the rule she had worked out. The teacher explained the textbook rule to her but let her decide which method to use in solving the problem.

Assignments given to children who are highly creative should frequently be open-ended. Instead of writing a book report, they could be asked to write another chapter for the book, perhaps one that carries the story forward. Instead of the traditional social studies lessons, there could be dramatic improvisation or role-playing as a way of learning about other people.

The teachers should provide gifted youngsters with a great deal of independent work. They should encourage the children to pursue their own interests and allow them enough freedom and time to finish their own projects their own way.

Good teachers avoid sexism and other stereotypes. They hold the same expectations, and provide the same educational opportunities, for boys and girls alike. They avoid prejudice against minority or culturally disadvantaged youth. And they pay as much attention to performance in social and artistic activities as they do to academic achievements and IQ score.

These teachers also have a broad range of teaching strategies. They are able to get children who are interested only in math to think logically about material they find in books and newspapers. They can introduce children who are interested only in music to a foreign language. The good teacher of the gifted understands how children learn and is able to select the best teaching style and the best materials for each child's abilities, interests, and way of thinking.

Generally speaking, successful teachers of the gifted are skilled in both scholarly and artistic pursuits, have wide interests, and exhibit a good sense of humor. They are usually student-centered, enthusiastic about teaching, and interested in advanced study for themselves.

Research shows that much talent and ability among the gifted goes unrecognized and unrewarded. Teachers often do not create opportunities that allow gifted children to use their skills or to show their talents to others. They do not encourage the gifted to explore subject matter in terms of values, morality, and social significance.

One group of bright six- to eight-year-olds in Michigan did an independent study on the dragonfly. Their teacher showed the results to some state officials. In time, this led to the dragonfly becoming the state insect of Michigan. In another instance, two advanced high school science students in Connecticut did a study of wind patterns near a reservoir. On the basis of their report, the location of a proposed highway was changed to avoid polluting the water.

Gifted children need to be accepted by their parents, teachers, and friends. At the same time they need to be helped to learn and to achieve. It is up to the parents and the education system working together to see that the gifted receive both a good feeling about themselves and the satisfaction of success.

Several of the attitudes and skills necessary for good teaching of the gifted are covered in the checklist below. If you think you are gifted, study this list carefully, as you did the Parent Checklist earlier. Then discuss it with your teachers.

TEACHER CHECKLIST

1. Are your teachers enthusiastic about teaching?
2. Do they ask you questions that lead you to learn for yourself?
3. Do they help you develop reasoning and thinking abilities?
4. Do they tell you where the facts are to be found and then let you collect them?
5. Do they help you formulate imaginative and creative ideas?

6. Do they encourage original research?
7. Do they exhibit more than one teaching style?
8. Do they let you try experiments in class?
9. Can they take criticism?
10. Can they say, "I don't know, but I can help you find out"?

Chapter 6
PROBLEMS OF THE GIFTED

While many gifted and talented children become very high achievers, up to half do not succeed. These youngsters do poorly in school, are socially isolated, and have other problems that interfere with fulfilling their potential.

Among the 400 prominent people in Goertzels' study, more than half said that they had hated school. They had performed poorly and had gotten low grades.

A study in Iowa showed that one out of every five of the state's gifted students did not complete high school. A Vermont report stated that many highly gifted children achieve only average or below-average results in school. And in a Pennsylvania study it was found that 80 percent of the children recommended for the testing of emotional disorders were children with IQs over 130.

Why don't all gifted and talented youngsters do well in school?

SENSE OF DIFFERENCE

Eight-year-old Gloria is a second-grader. She has a mental age of fourteen. Gloria can talk about the world situation or the American economy with ease. But at the same time, it is not unusual for her to climb into her mother's lap to be cuddled.

Gloria's behavior typifies the chief problem that most gifted children face. It is a "sense of difference." The difficulty stems from the fact that their outstanding talent or superior intellectual development may be out of step with their emotional and social development.

These children may think and speak like older children, but socially, physically, and emotionally they are usually more like children of their own age. Also, many gifted children have especially acute senses of taste and smell and stronger than normal reactions to colors and shapes. If their differences are accepted by those around them, the youngsters grow up accepting their giftedness. If not, these differences may disturb the child, and later, the adult.

POOR SELF-CONCEPT

Gregory is a seven-year-old who does not want to go to school. Both of his parents teach college. At the age of three, Gregory learned to read by himself.

As soon as Gregory's parents realized he was gifted, they made a big fuss over him. They paid a lot of attention to him when he read, and showed him off to their friends. Otherwise, though, they spent very little time with him.

Sometimes parents of children who show early signs of giftedness expect too much from their children. They place great value on the child's accomplishments before the child has developed confidence in his or her own intelligence. They talk a great deal about school and grades. They push the child to do more than he or she is ready to do. These children sometimes grow up feeling that their parents are more interested in what they can do than in who they are.

Other parents may be threatened by the fact that their child has unusual abilities. They may reject the child or make insulting remarks. Perhaps they use such nicknames as "smarty," "brainy," or "egghead."

Some children, like Gregory, enter school with a poor sense of self. These children do not like themselves. They lack confidence and do not trust their ability to achieve.

Gifted children can also develop self-concept problems in school. These children usually come to school eager and willing to learn. But soon they begin to hate school because it does not meet their needs. The problem shows up when they fail to achieve. This displeases their teachers and parents. Then, they may not get along with the other children. They begin to feel like outsiders in the classroom. This may lead to anxiety and fearfulness. A lack of friendship with others may hamper their later social and psychological development.

BORED AND FRUSTRATED

Rachel spoke well at an early age. She learned easily and had a rich vocabulary. Although she did well in the first three grades of school, her work began to slip in the fourth grade.

Rachel had begun to form bad habits in first grade when she finished her work ahead of everyone else. Her attention wandered. She doodled in the margins of her workbooks. It was very frustrating for her to move at the same pace as the other children.

Before long she wasn't paying any attention in class. She did barely enough to get by. Now she is far behind most of the other fourth-graders. She does poorly in school because she never mastered the basic skills.

Children like Rachel develop poor learning patterns and bad study habits in school. Their attendance often drops. Patterns established early are very difficult to change later on.

Bored children sometimes become troublemakers. They are unruly in school and disrupt the classroom. Even though they may be punished for it, their poor behavior at least helps to relieve the boredom. Sometimes they lash out at those they blame for their discomfort. They argue every point with the teacher. They become cruel and nasty to the other children. They create tension at home.

There are many accounts of talented and gifted individuals who underachieved in school, quite possibly because of boredom. Both Thomas Edison and Albert Einstein were considered dull by their teachers. The great Russian pianist and composer Sergei Rachmaninoff got such poor grades on his report card from the music conservatory that he had to cheat to graduate. And Pablo Picasso failed at school because he refused to do anything but paint.

NONCONFORMITY

Fred loved drawing and painting. But his teachers thought he should be interested in science and math, not in art. They tried to discourage him from working with art materials.

Jenny was a slow, deliberate thinker. In school and at home, she was always being rushed or interrupted by adults who wanted her to give quick, glib answers.

Herb had far more ability in science than anyone else in his class in junior high school. He wanted to go ahead on his own, but his teachers would not allow it.

Pablo Picasso as a young man.

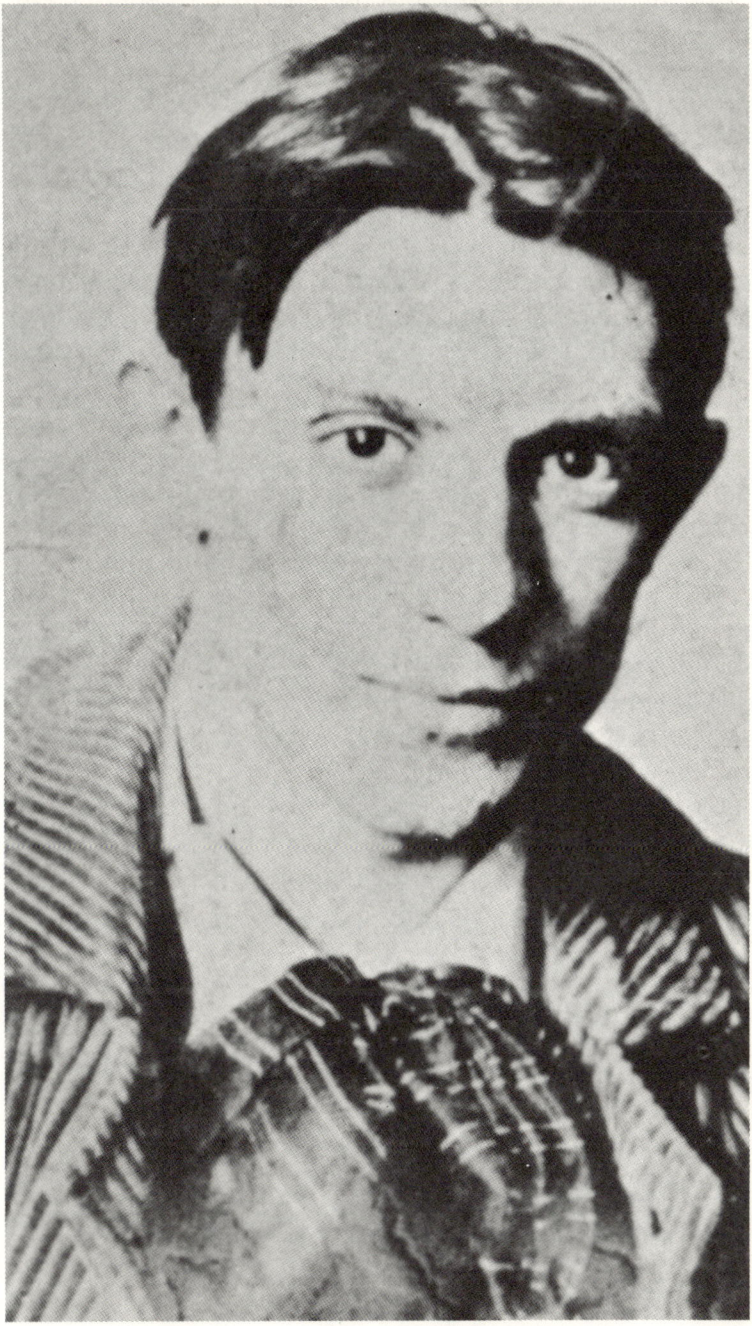

Children like Fred and Jenny are particularly creative. The main trait of people who are creative is that they are original. To be original is to go against the usual way of doing things.

Highly creative youngsters are often the most different from the average. They are frequently made to feel embarrassed because their special gifts seem strange and hard to understand to the teachers and children around them. Often their creative behavior is regarded as aggressive or hostile. Some hide their abilities and learn to conform. They become very ordinary students in school. Others resent school and drop out because school just gets in their way.

Highly academic youngsters like Herb are even more likely to be damaged by poor experiences in school. Since they are praised for finishing first, they learn to rush through their work. But by rushing they often fail to sharpen their abilities or broaden their scope. The result is success in the classroom without really trying and without really learning how to study or how to think.

In a New York study on underachievers, "conforming teachers" and "conforming schools" were held most to blame for underachievement among middle-class and upper middle-class pupils. The "angry teacher," who is sarcastic, belittling, suspicious, and quick to criticize; the "bored teacher," who is not interested in the subject or the students; the "easily satisfied teacher," who is willing to settle for second-best; and the "rigid teacher," who does not provide for individual differences, were found to be the most harmful teacher types.

ISOLATION

Mark is a serious student. He is very shy and quiet. At school he does average work. But at home he has built a citizen's band radio and a telescope and has installed an intercom system. Mark much prefers adults to people his own age.

Signs of extraordinary ability and an early show of creativity sometimes can separate and isolate children like Mark from other children. Knowing that they are "different" can be very lonely and frightening. When they are at school, some gifted children try to overcome this by acting as close to average and ordinary as possible.

Research shows that gifted children who are not happy in school often sleep less than normal. It has been demonstrated that youngsters with an IQ of 160 or higher have little or no social life. Often they reject friendships in order to assert their own individuality. As E. Paul Torrance said, their greatest problem is coping with the effects of being a "minority of one."

SEX DISCRIMINATION

Gifted children are sometimes forced to live up to certain behavioral standards associated with social and sex roles. About half of all gifted boys and a quarter of all gifted girls are considered educational underachievers. The boys usually begin their pattern of underachievement in the early grades, girls in the upper grades and in junior high school. The pressure to conform to sex roles creates adjustment problems for these potential high achievers. Gifted children, apparently, often tailor their abilities in order to fit society's notion of what boys should do and what girls should do.

A recent study pinpointed the effect of society's expectations on children. A group of seventh-grade gifted girls showed a great deal of interest in science and math, as well as in culture and the arts. A similar group of girls in the ninth grade, however, showed much less interest in science and math while maintaining the same interest in culture and the arts. The explanation offered is that these girls received the message, between seventh and ninth grade, that girls should be more interested in the arts than in science or math.

The fact is that boys outnumber girls two to one in gifted programs. Gifted boys and girls of equal ability and from similar backgrounds, for example, do not achieve equally in mathematics. More boys than girls have been identified as outstanding in mathematics at a young age, though they both seem to show the same potential for development.

Evidence suggests that scientific and mathematical achievement are closely connected to interests and values. If society values only males as scientists and mathematicians, then girls will tend to channel their energies in different directions. It is hard for anyone to succeed in these fields without the help and encouragement of family, teachers, friends, and society at large.

What is an underachiever made of?

Dr. E. Paul Torrance has written: "A scorned imagination, an unused memory, tabooed sensations, an interrupted thought, a rejected question, a forbidden daydream, an unexpressed idea, an unsought judgment, an unpainted picture, an unsung song, a safely hidden poem, unused talents. . . . These make an underachiever."

Chapter 7
TESTING FOR GIFTEDNESS

Throughout the school years, students are tested on what they have learned, on what they should learn, and on how fast they may be expected to learn.

Testing for giftedness is particularly difficult. Do you test for academic giftedness? For creative giftedness? For talent? How do you take into account the many variations in inborn ability, learned ability, thinking ability, physical development, and personality?

The purpose of all tests is to get an estimate of a person's potential. Where children are involved, a particular child's test score is usually compared with the test scores earned by a large number of other children the same age. This gives the tester an estimate of the child's abilities. Test scores often play a large part in identifying a child as gifted or talented.

TESTS OF LEARNING ABILITY: IQ

Choose the word that makes this sentence true:

Bird is to feather as dog is to
(1) bark, (2) tail, (3) paw, (4) fur.

Choose the one word that does not belong with the others:

(1) dog, (2) horse, (3) cat, (4) chicken, (5) cow.

What is the next number in this series:
1—3—9—27?

(1) 30, (2) 33, (3) 45, (4) 81, (5) 243.

Which of the following activities is *not* work?

(1) playing baseball, (2) chopping wood, (3) washing dishes, (4) typing, (5) driving a car.

These are some typical types of questions from tests of learning ability. Such tests are often called IQ tests, or academic aptitude tests. Since it is impossible to get inside a person's mind to measure brightness, these tests are used to measure a person's ability to solve intellectual problems. This ability is considered by some to be an estimate of the person's intelligence.

Intelligence actually consists of many different abilities. The IQ test is only able to measure certain of these abilities. It is largely a test of the ability to do convergent thinking. This is the kind of thinking about which most people converge, or agree. Convergent thinking, for example, applies to the meanings of words, the answers to math problems, and to most facts and figures.

IQ scores are not always reliable indicators of intelligence. While the score is never higher than a child's level of functioning, it may be as much as thirty points below. Illness or an emotional problem, such as fear of the examiner or fear of the test, may lower the score. Cultural differences, too, influence the results.

John, who lives in a lower-class neighborhood, lost several points in the vocabulary section of an IQ test because he said that *fuzz* is a policeman, *lark* is the name of a cigarette, and *bread* is another word for money. He is correct according to the language he hears and uses. But he is wrong according to the testers.

Nadia's family recently came to the United States from the Soviet Union. Her parents speak only Russian at home. She did poorly on an IQ test because she still does not understand English very well.

Alex, a fifth-grader, scored below average on an IQ test. Yet he is able to read on a ninth-grade level. He would have scored much higher if his parents had provided some informal learning at home. Alex was never at a zoo, a movie, a concert, or a museum. He never visited a farm, a factory, or a department store. There are no books or newspapers in his home. All of his learning takes place in school or comes from the library books he reads. He does not have the experience and background to do well on IQ tests.

There are other problems with IQ tests. Some, such as those for children below the age of six, are of little use. Others have a top limit to what they can measure. This limit is sometimes too low to discriminate between the above average, the gifted, and the highly gifted.

Also, the multiple-choice format limits the children to certain answers. To the gifted individual, who has greater insights and can see beyond the obvious, all the answers may seem wrong. Or some of the wrong answers may actually seem right. For instance, in the last question of the sample given, a gifted student might realize that all the activities could be work or leisure, depending on the exact situation.

For these reasons, many school systems no longer use standardized IQ tests to measure their students' learning abilities. The New York City schools, for example, have given up IQ tests entirely. But a good number of educators still believe that IQ scores are useful tools in getting a picture of a youngster's mental capacity. Where IQs are used as a measure of giftedness, an IQ of 120 is usually considered the lowest figure of the gifted range. For some programs an IQ of 125 or 130 may be used.

ACHIEVEMENT TESTS

Divide 448 by 16.

List the state capitals of Ohio, California, Texas, New York, and Maine.

Give the chemical formula for water.

These are typical questions from achievement tests. Achievement tests measure specific information skills and ideas that are taught in school. These tests measure how well students have learned the subjects they have studied. There are achievement tests in all subjects, including reading, math, social studies, science, and foreign languages.

Many achievement tests are given to groups or entire classes of children rather than to individuals. Several factors may interfere here, resulting in a score that is lower than a child's day-to-day performance. Group tests very often yield results below those of individual tests. Also, achievement tests are not able to identify the gifted child who is underachieving, the creatively gifted child, or the talented child. The tests only measure achievement in schoolwork.

Gifted children, though, usually do well on achievement tests. They often score two to three grades above their age level. In general, educators have found that high reading achievement and high math achievement are related to superior intelligence.

TESTS OF CREATIVITY

Imagine that you just received a new bicycle, but it came in many pieces. What things could you make from the pieces, other than a bicycle?

What would happen if everyone always told the truth about everything?

What would happen if the oceans dried up?

List as many things in the shape of a square as you can think of.

These are the types of questions found in tests of creativity. Tests of creativity measure divergent thinking, which is very different from the convergent thinking measured by IQ tests. Divergent thinking is thinking that goes off in different directions. It is not thinking that is generally agreed on. Creative thinking ability, then, is different from general intelligence.

Tests for creativity were developed because fundamental differences were found between those people who are highly intelligent and those people who are highly creative. While creative behavior occurs in persons of high intelligence, high intelligence alone does not insure creativity.

Many of the most important aspects of creativity are not measured by the usual IQ tests. Only one out of every four top scorers on creativity tests scores in the upper 20 percent on IQ tests. Many score IQs of 120, or slightly less. Therefore large numbers of highly creative children are not included in special programs for the gifted that use only IQ scores.

In 1961, J. W. Getzels and P. W. Jackson published a classic study, *Creativity and Intelligence,* on the relationship between creativity and IQ score. They found that high scorers on creativity tests achieved as well in school as high scorers on IQ tests. In another study, researchers found that when both IQ and creativity scores were high, students did well academically. But when IQ scores dropped below 120, individuals sometimes had academic difficulties.

Some of the best known tests for creativity are the Torrance Tests of Creative Thinking, devised by Dr. E. Paul Torrance. The tests cover four areas of creativity:

1. The ability to produce many ideas in response to a stimulus, or fluency.
2. The ability to produce different kinds of ideas, or flexibility.
3. The ability to produce unusual ideas, or originality.
4. The ability to add details to an idea, or elaboration.

Other creativity tests cover two more areas:

5. The ability to combine two or more ideas, or synthesis.
6. The ability to delay completion of a task to allow time for new ideas, or closure.

The chief problem with these tests is that since there are no "correct" answers, the scoring depends very much on the tester. What may seem like a bright and original idea to one person may appear to be without merit to another.

Another danger, too, is that the test may be too narrow. Jean, a young girl with a gift for musical composition, did very poorly on a creativity test that was mostly concerned with solving mechanical problems, such as the one above dealing with the bicycle.

Sometimes a school will measure creativity by examining a student's creative work or by having authorities in the field judge the work. Studies have

1. _____ 2. _____

3. _____ 4. _____

The test on this page is similar to the Torrance Tests of Creative Thinking. The test-taker is asked to add lines to the incomplete figures and make an interesting picture. A colorful title is to be written at the bottom of each block next to the number of the figure.

shown that students who show signs of creativity in high school usually continue their creative accomplishments through college and beyond.

Another tool used to identify creativity in children is the biographical inventory. Here the children answer questions about their lives—their families, interests and hobbies, most enjoyable activities, outstanding experiences, favorite books, (movies, TV shows), and so on. Such inventories help to identify students with strong academic skills, leadership ability, and creativity in music or art. Sometimes other tests are used later to make more specific and accurate measurements of the giftedness or talent.

BEHAVIOR-RATING SCALES

Behavior-rating scales measure ability by carefully watching students perform in normal situations. The scales provide guidelines on what to look for. The tester rates a student's behavior using terms such as *always, sometimes,* or *never.* Among the usual items being observed are: Is the student able to follow written instructions? Is he or she able to follow oral instructions? Does the student persist at a task until it is completed? Does he or she ask for help? Is the child able to accept failure?

Each factor is given a certain numerical value. The total score is a measure of the child's giftedness. These behavior-rating scales are particularly valuable in identifying gifted youngsters who score low on standardized tests.

TEACHER SELECTION

Identification by teachers is one of the most widely used methods of locating gifted children. It is also one of the most limited.

Most studies show that teachers are not able to identify gifted children very well. In one study teachers were right only 50 percent of the time. In fact, they identified as gifted many students who were in the average range on IQ tests. In another study, teachers of very young children identified only 10 percent of the gifted children in their classes.

Teachers may fail to identify the gifted because of their concern for groups of children and averages. They may be more interested in academic skills, and factors such as neatness. Some teachers prefer stuents who do not ask too many questions, especially when the questions do not deal directly with the topic under discussion. Since the gifted often reach beyond the issues at hand, make leaps in logic, and pursue thoughts further than most students and teachers, their answers are often viewed as either disruptive or incorrect. In short, they may be punished for their giftedness and receive poor grades for their work.

Teachers also often base their judgments on impressions. So, they may tend to overrate factors such as attractiveness, liveliness, and verbosity, and pass over students who are nonverbal or rebellious. Bright girls in the elementary grades, for example, are usually marked higher than bright boys, since they are often more socially conforming.

PARENT SELECTION

Some people think that all parents consider their children gifted and talented. Therefore, they say, parents should be the last ones to ask if their children are gifted. Yet according to recent research, parents show excellent judgment in identifying the gifted and talented.

A study in Rockford, Illinois, examined parental ability to recognize giftedness in their own kindergarten children. Parents correctly selected 67 percent of gifted kindergartners. Teachers selected only 22 percent. Also, parents tended to overestimate the children's abilities less often than did the teachers.

Parental views are especially useful when they are based at least partly on anecdotal information about their gifted children. These anecdotes frequently point up early giftedness better than tests, impartial observations, or any other method known.

PEER NOMINATION

Peer nomination is now getting more attention as a useful factor in selecting children for gifted and talented programs. Classmates are asked such questions as: Who would you ask to help you with a math problem? Who knows the answers to most questions? Who is the most way-out thinker in the class?

Members of selection committees in certain school districts were asked to indicate the value of different types of data in identifying gifted youngsters for special programs. Peer nomination received the highest usefulness rating. It was also considered to be the type of information that most helped the total group arrive at decisions.

Standardized tests are very common ways to identify gifted and talented students. But since every child is a complex being, with many strengths and weaknesses, the new approach is to use data from many different sources to get as complete a picture of the total child as possible.

The case study approach uses many factors to identify giftedness. These include self-evaluation (including biographical information), peer nomination, parent selection, teacher observations, as well as creativity test results, achievement test results, and IQ scores.

The case study approach appears to be better able to identify youngsters with unusual backgrounds. As the number of programs for gifted youngsters continues to grow, it is important to have an identification system that takes into account all types of differences in people.

Chapter 8
PROGRAMS FOR THE GIFTED

"In our class, it's cool to be smart."
"Here we go into things deeply."
"In my school I can practice the piano three hours a day."
"I'm working on a science project in my high school that may be a cure for cancer some day."

This is what four gifted and talented students have to say about their special education programs. They belong to a small but growing number of students in programs that are based on special capabilities and the real differences in the way the gifted learn.

The goals for education of the gifted and talented are the same as for all children. But the key reason for special programs is to provide the different experiences and different opportunities the gifted need. This may mean providing work in areas not usually explored by the average child or encouraging the use of more sophisticated ways of thinking than are usually taught.

There are three basic approaches to the education of children who are gifted and talented. One educates the children in separate classes or separate schools. Another places the students in regular classes but allows them to skip some grades and subjects, thereby moving them through school faster than others. And the third educates the gifted in regular classes but gives them opportunities inside the classroom and out to explore various subjects in greater depth.

SELF-CONTAINED CLASSES: BIRDS OF A FEATHER

In self-contained classes for children who are gifted and talented the teacher is specially trained to work with the youngsters at their proper mental age, whatever their chronological age. The belief is that the students benefit from instruction designed to meet their particular needs and also from being with other gifted children.

A number of self-contained classes exist within regular schools, but there are also separate schools only for the gifted. Some schools offer part-time programs that take the gifted students out of their regular classes part of each week. Other programs offer classes that meet only during the summer or on weekends.

For over thirty years the Cleveland public school system has had a program that provides for the gifted a number of self-contained groups called Major Work classes. Any student who scores high in certain achievement tests, has an IQ of 125 or above, and is nominated by parents and teachers may be placed in a Major Work class.

The focus in these classes is on developing each child's initiative, creativity, and sense of responsibility. There are individual and group projects. The youngsters have group discussions led by a discussion leader who changes each time. The work is much like the work done in regular classrooms, but its quality, according to some observers, is much higher. Special features of this program include a concentration on music, art, and creative writing, as well as lessons in typing and French.

The Bronx High School of Science in New York City accepts 600 students each year who are identified as gifted by their high scores on mathematics and science achievement tests. Most were in honors courses in junior high school. One part of the program has fifty tenth-graders meeting together for ten periods a week. They use this time for extra laboratory work and for pursuing individual research problems.

The Astor Program for Gifted Children, sponsored by the New York City school system, is an example of a part-time program. Children with IQ scores of 130 and over are eligible. The main focus here is on the development of leadership skills. The Astor Program believes that leadership ability is tied to the quality of a child's imagination. It strives to develop each child's imagination through the use of various techniques, from block play to dramatization.

The Governor's School in Salem, North Carolina, gathers gifted students from all over the state for special summer programs in various academic areas. Horizons Unlimited in Keene, New Hampshire, provides activities which foster creative and productive abilities in its gifted students. The Talcott Mountain Science Program in Avon, Connecticut, provides weekend projects for students with particular gifts in science.

Research shows that not all self-contained programs increase the child's potential for success. Those that present the same curriculum taught in regular classes, or use traditional methods of teaching, are of little value. But where the gifted and talented students have different courses of study and different instruction and materials, they derive important benefits.

Gifted children need interaction with other gifted children on a regular basis, but they also need interaction with ordinary children. Self-contained programs are contrary to current efforts to mainstream—return to the regular classroom to the fullest extent possible—all youngsters. Only when it is financially impossible to do otherwise is the government now supporting segregated programs.

ACCELERATED PROGRAMS: MORE SCHOOLING, LESS TIME

Accelerated programs allow children to move through an educational system faster than usual. This approach is based on the idea that certain children can learn faster and absorb more than others in a given period.

Most acceleration programs either admit youngsters to kindergarten, high school, or college at an earlier age than usual or, once in, they permit them to skip certain grades or subjects. Sometimes acceleration involves a combination of both.

Since 1971, Johns Hopkins University in Baltimore, Maryland, has had a program of accepting students who are outstanding in science and mathematics. Tests on the eleventh- or twelfth-grade level are given to seventh- and eighth-graders. About one percent of the students taking these tests score high enough to be considered genuinely gifted in math and science.

These very young, very bright students are able to enter the university. When they arrive, they are treated like other college students. They do not form a separate group. A local Baltimore youngster, Joseph

Bates, was admitted to Hopkins from the eighth grade. Eight years later he received a Doctor of Philosophy degree from Cornell University. Michael Kotschenreuther entered Hopkins from the ninth grade. He studied theoretical physics and got a Doctor of Philosophy degree from Princeton University a few years later.

The advantage here is that these accelerated students are able to start their careers early. One research study shows that outstanding scientists and mathematicians do their most productive work between twenty and thirty years of age. Another shows a close connection between earning an advanced college degree at a young age and professional success. Programs similar to the one at Hopkins now exist in Minnesota, with others springing up in Illinois, Indiana, Michigan, and Oklahoma.

A 1938 study compared students who entered the University of California at age sixteen and a half or younger, with those who entered at age seventeen or older. The accelerated group was ahead in grade average, number of scholarships, and number of academic awards. They held more class offices and took part in more school activities.

The greatest number of behavior problems was found in two groups, bright students who were not accelerated and students of average intelligence who were accelerated. A more recent study compared two groups of gifted children. One group had been accelerated in elementary school, the other group had not. The results were similar to the California research.

The major objection to acceleration is that it does not allow gifted children to grow up with people of their own age. Acceleration seems to work best with gifted individuals who are socially and emotionally mature, as well as intellectually superior. It is much more valuable for the truly gifted than for bright or above-average students. And it is only successful when it builds on the learning needs of the students in the program, not just on rapid movement through the grades.

ENRICHMENT: RICHER FARE FOR FASTER LEARNERS

Enrichment is what occurs when gifted children stay in regular classrooms but are given independent projects, special activities, and other supplementary work to deepen their studies.

Quite often an enrichment program of independent study is based on a written contract between the student and the teacher. The contract calls for a certain amount of work to be accomplished within a certain period of time. In addition to the usual teaching methods, enrichment programs may use separate resource teachers or a team-teaching approach. A resource room is equipped with materials not usually found in regular classrooms, such as computer and TV teaching devices and special learning kits. The team-teaching approach allows children to draw on the expertise of more than one teacher.

Mentor programs also provide enrichment for children who are gifted. This approach pairs a gifted youngster with an expert in a field that is of interest to the youngster. The federal government, for example, is funding one program in which youngsters talk with authors or others around the country via radio and headphones.

In one mentor program in the state of California, a gifted high school senior spends several hours a week with the chief planner for the local bus company. A mentor program in New York has top students on the high school level working twice a week with gifted students in an elementary school. Two of the present group are excellent math students. They help three gifted kindergartners to learn winning board game strategies. Another high school mentor, an expert in computer programming, teaches computer science to four bright third-graders.

George Washington University Reading Center in Washington, D.C., has an after-school enrichment program for gifted youngsters in grades three through eight. The after-school program provides for gifted and talented students without isolating them from their peers during the school day. Some of the subjects covered in this program include a study of Shakespeare's plays, architecture, and poetry. The idea is to build higher-level thinking skills through experiences with literature, drama, and other cultural arts.

At best, enrichment programs add breadth and depth to gifted children's understanding of basic subjects. They go beyond routine memorization of facts. This approach takes advantage of special characteristics of the gifted, such as the ability to draw generalizations, to pursue topics in depth, and to use initiative, imagination, and originality.

At their worst, enrichment programs merely offer the gifted child busywork, such as copying pages out of a book or doing large numbers of similar math problems. This sort of thing kills, rather than encourages, initiative and creativity. Some enrichment programs are below the level of the students and do not offer them enough of a challenge. Other times teachers provide a variety of interesting activities but without any order, direction, or clear goals in mind.

INDIVIDUALIZED EDUCATION PROGRAMS—IEPs

Some states, including Pennsylvania, Idaho, Florida, and North Carolina, are now developing Individualized Education Programs (IEPs) for the academically gifted. In these states, an IEP is written for each exceptional child.

The IEP takes into account the unique learning needs of the child. It suggests the program best suited to each student's giftedness. In some cases it means placement in a self-contained program; for others, a regular class with certain modifications is more appropriate.

What should a good IEP for the gifted contain?

1. The program should be geared toward the development of higher-level thinking skills.
2. The program should develop the child's abilities in a logical, orderly way.
3. The program should take into consideration the interests of the student, as well as information from parents, teachers, and other professionals, to provide a balanced program for the child.
4. The program should set goals and should measure progress in particular areas of ability.

All students need appropriate learning situations that are challenging and stimulating. School should not be a time of frustration or boredom. But for the gifted, in particular, the most appropriate education is often a program that encourages the development of advanced thinking skills, creativity, problem-solving skills, and inquisitiveness.

Commissioner of Education Sidney Marland put it this way: "Gifted and talented youth are a unique population, different markedly from their age peers in abilities, interests and psychological maturity. They are the most versatile and complex of all human groups...."

The gifted and talented are also the most neglected of all groups with special educational needs. We can hope that, as the facts about the gifted and talented become better known, many more programs of all kinds will be set up throughout the country.

Chapter 9
THE DISADVANTAGED GIFTED

The potential for giftedness is the same for all children, no matter what their ethnic, economic, religious, or social background. The ingredients for success are also the same. Yet, the fact is that there are far too few children from poor homes in programs for the gifted.

The disadvantaged, according to one definition, include all who do not share in the material, economic, and educational benefits that are enjoyed by the majority.

Being disadvantaged causes particular difficulties for potentially gifted and talented students. Research shows that the performance of disadvantaged students steadily decreases from primary to intermediate grades. Today, large numbers of gifted children, who happen to be disadvantaged, are not recognized and not provided for.

Why are the disadvantaged not achieving more? What steps are being taken to identify and educate children with exceptional abilities from disadvantaged backgrounds?

PROBLEMS

Pauline is an eleven-year-old fifth-grader. She lives in a rundown slum neighborhood in Cleveland. She is interested in school, but each year she falls further and further behind in her work. Her life at home is very unpleasant. Her mother and father are always fighting and arguing. There is seldom enough money to pay the rent and buy food. Pauline comes to school in worn, ill-fitting clothes. Although she seems to have a high potential as an artist, neither her parents nor her teachers encourage her to develop that talent.

Many potentially gifted and talented children like Pauline, from unfavorable home environments, enter school expecting to fail. Discrimination by society at large causes a poor sense of self-worth and feelings of anger and frustration. Some of the failures may be self-fulfilled prophecies. Neither children nor parents nor teachers expect disadvantaged children to have superior ability in many cases. Also, many disadvantaged youngsters have learned to distrust authority figures or to regard them as enemies.

Another frequent problem is a lack of motivation. Disadvantaged children usually have so many day-to-day difficulties—personal safety in high-crime areas, a never-ending shortage of money, food, and clothing, an unstable family structure—that it is hard for them to fix on distant goals. Often the insensitivity of teachers and others to these problems cause the children to feel alienated. Poor nutrition may lead to low energy levels and limit the children's activities in school.

Lack of proper stimulation is yet another problem commonly associated with children from poor socioeconomic backgrounds. The families seldom encourage the children to read, write, draw pictures, or develop hobbies. Often there are no books, magazines, scrap paper, or pictures in the home for the child to look at or use.

Disadvantaged youngsters who achieve below their abilities often have specific learning difficulties. A limited vocabulary due to poor speech models at home, little respect for learning and education, little help or encouragement from parents, and no privacy in crowded and noisy home conditions may all interfere with developing skills.

These children often enter school with poor experiential backgrounds. They have had few contacts with people who would exchange ideas with them, answer their questions, or take them to places of interest. Male figures are frequently missing from the home.

Without money, opportunities to make choices and to learn how to make decisions are limited. Children who cannot play safely outdoors cannot develop as well physically and socially as those who can. When there is limited transportation, children cannot always get to special after-school programs.

Poor families tend to move more often than middle-class families. The family unit may change, with new people coming and going. Meals are often informal affairs, and seldom does the entire family eat together. Children for whom English is a second language have the additional problem of communicating outside the home.

Research has shown that the higher the social and economic status of the family the higher the IQ of the children. Parents in the professions and in top business jobs tend to have more high-IQ children, and the reverse is true. Among the reasons given are the better education of the parents, the superior schooling the children usually receive, and the many extra cultural advantages that are provided. Only 6 percent of children who live in slum conditions score a 125 IQ or higher; 25 percent of children who live in suburban areas score above this level.

Commissioner of Education Sidney Marland, in his 1972 Report on the Gifted and Talented, urged early identification of minority gifted and talented children. He cited evidence showing that unfavorable social and educational environments suppress most children's potential to a point where it cannot be recognized in the later years. The 1978 law mentioned earlier authorizes special funds to discover the potentially gifted and talented among disadvantaged children.

TESTING

Testing for gifted and talented children from disadvantaged homes is very difficult. Most tests for giftedness have been prepared and standardized for groups of middle-class or upper-class children. What is not taken into account is the fact that many children today come from non-English speaking or culturally different homes.

Researchers have recently created new ways to identify gifted young people from culturally different backgrounds. These tests do not assume that everyone shares the same cultural background and the same mastery of English.

The so-called culture-fair tests stress non-verbal items. They are an attempt to circumvent the problems gifted children from different cultural backgrounds have with the verbal and language items on most tests. The Torrance Tests of Creative Thinking, for example, are largely free of cultural associations. Individuals from disadvantaged groups, it is found, perform as well on these tests as those from non-disadvantaged groups.

Some experts depend on biographical inventories, anecdotal records, and teacher observation to identify disadvantaged gifted children. Some success has also been reported with self-recommendations and recommendations by other children. Often children will recommend students that the teachers would not have selected. These are later found to be excellent choices.

Many programs also use parent selection to identify the gifted, though culturally different, child. A study of the Mexican-American gifted done by E. Bernal showed that parents are quite good at identifying potentially gifted children. In Houston, Texas, in addition to asking parents for recommendations, there are TV and radio appeals to try to find eligible children in the community.

The Baldwin-Identification Matrix (BIM) is a very popular method of identifying the gifted. It is especially useful in locating gifted and talented youngsters in disadvantaged areas. BIM collects data from standardized IQ and achievement tests, along with several other tests, to get a complete picture of the child. The other tests cover all areas of giftedness: intelligence, academic achievement, creativity, talent in art, music, and drama, as well as leadership skills. BIM gives a child from a different cultural background a fair chance to be chosen for a special program.

Bernal's report on Mexican-American gifted children summed up the most important facts in identifying disadvantaged gifted. It pointed out that all children are unique and that the gifted will not all be one type of child. By using the case study approach to find them, which includes a variety of methods, more of the different types of gifted children can be placed in classes for the gifted.

PROGRAMS

Programs for disadvantaged gifted children are aimed first at identifying ability. They then try to help to raise the children's self-understanding.

One way to accomplish this is to help children focus on their abilities. The children can be made aware of who they are and where they are going. As the teacher of one inner-city school said: "These

Baldwin Identification Matrix (BIM)

ADAPTED FOR USE BY: Gifted Talented Screening Committee   DATE 5/79
STUDENT: Susan Matrix   SCHOOL: Longsworth Elementary
AGE 9   GRADE 3   SEX F   SCHOOL DISTRICT: Waverly

ASSESSMENT ITEMS	5	4	3	2	1	B-NA
1. Cognitive Abilities Test	140+	139-130 ✓	129-120	119-110	109-100	
2. Metropolitan Achievement Reading	95%ile ✓	94-90%ile	89-85%ile	84-80%ile	79-75%ile	
3. Metropolitan Achievement Math	sta. 9	8 ✓	7	6	5	
4. Renzulli Leadership	40	39-35	34-30	29-25 ✓	24-20	
5. Renzulli Creativity	40	39-35	34-30 ✓	29-25	24-20	
6. In-school Psychomotor	5	4	3	2 ✓	1	
7. Renzulli Motivation	36-34	33-30 ✓	29-26	25-22	21-18	
8. Renzulli Learning	32	31-28 ✓	27-24	23-20	19-16	
9. Teacher recommendation	5 ✓	4	3	2	1	
10.						
11.						
COLUMN TALLY OF CHECKS	2	4	1	2	0	
WEIGHT	×5	×4	×3	×2	×1	
ADD ACROSS	10 +	16 +	3 +	4 +	0	=

TOTAL SCORE: **33**

© 1977   OVER →

children are going to be scholars and professionals. They are going to be the teachers someday." The gifted pupils at this school spend a part of each day in various specialty classes such as drama, Spanish, photography, journalism, science, instrumental music, or advanced math.

What some might consider disadvantages, the "gifted" teacher in these programs regards as virtues. One teacher tells her bilingual pupils: "Think how lucky you are—you know two languages." And she bases a lot of her instruction on the rich culture that is part of the ethnic backgrounds of the children in the class.

Dr. Torrance's program to help the disadvantaged gifted, especially in areas of creativity, stresses activities such as brainstorming. A teacher once started off a brainstorming session by asking the children to find out how many different ways peanut butter could be used. They finally agreed that there are about twenty-five different ways—besides spreading it on bread. One young man, for instance, discovered that it could be used as glue. Looking at ordinary things in new ways develops creativity. The teachers also provide new and unfamiliar experiences to broaden the children's outlook.

One four-part program for working with the disadvantaged gifted revolves around occupational goals. First, students explore and plan occupational goals with some help from the teacher. Next, they work with individuals from the community, examining specific occupations in depth. Third, parents work with the teacher to understand their own feelings and attitudes about their children's future plans. And fourth, the students are evaluated, and those that have done well are rewarded.

One seventeen-year-old inner-city black youngster, Maritza, hadn't been doing too well in her studies at a New Haven, Connecticut, high school. She was tested as part of a program aimed at identifying disadvantaged young people from culturally diverse backgrounds. The results showed that, in spite of low achievement in her regular studies, Maritza had creativity and real potential in acting.

Maritza, along with forty-five other youngsters in the area, started studying at the American Shakespeare Theatre Center. She goes there now for two two-and-a-half-hour sessions each week. The Center helps the children develop their acting abilities through improvisation and games that call for observation, concentration, and ingenuity.

One phase of the Center's work has to do with transformations. For example, students are asked to translate a short play into a musical composition. They have to decide how to transform the story and the action of the play into the rhythms, melodies, and harmonies of music. Such activities aid thinking, reading, and writing skills, as well.

With the Center program, Maritza has improved in her schoolwork, especially social studies, which has become her favorite subject. Although she is very enthusiastic about acting, she does not plan to become a professional actress. But the skills she is getting at the Center are giving her a new sense of confidence and an ability to communicate with ease.

To be young and gifted is difficult. To be young, gifted, and disadvantaged is even more difficult. But with proper guidance at home and special programs in school these difficulties can be overcome.

Bibliography

Gallagher, J., *Teaching the Gifted Child.* Second edition. Boston: Allyn, Bacon, Inc., 1975.

Goertzel, V. and Goertzel, M., *Cradles of Eminence,* New York: Little, Brown, 1962.

Gowan, J. C. and Torrance, E. P., *Educating the Ablest,* Itasca, Ill.: F. E. Peacock Publishers, Inc., 1971.

Grost, A., *Genius in Residence.* Englewood Cliffs, N.J.: Prentice Hall, 1970.

Guilford, J. P., *Intelligence, Creativity and Their Educational Implications.* Robert Knapp, 1968.

Hollingsworth, L., *Children Above 180 IQ Stanford Binet: Origins and Development,* Arno, 1977 (Reprint of 1942).

Krathwohl, D. R., Bloom, B. S., and Masia, B. B., *Taxonomy of Educational Objectives.* New York: David McKay, 1964.

Renzulli, J. S., *The Enrichment Triad Model: A Guide for Developing Defensible Programs for the Gifted and Talented.* Weathersfield, Conn.: Creative Learning Press, 1977.

Segal, J. and Yahraes, H., *A Child's Journey: Forces That Shape the Lives of Our Young.* New York: McGraw-Hill, 1978.

Strom, R. D. and Torrance, E. P., *Education for Effective Achievement.* Chicago: Rand McNally, 1973.

Terman, L. M., *The Gifted Child Grows Up: Twenty-Five Years. Follow-Up of a Superior Group.* California: Stanford University Press, 1959.

For Further Reading

Bigland, E., *Madame Curie*. New York: S. G. Philips, 1957.

Cabanne, P., *Pablo Picasso: A Biography*. New York, Morrow, 1977.

Clark, R. W., *Edison: The Man Who Made the Future*. New York: Putnam, 1977.

Ewin, D., *George Gershwin: His Journey to Greatness*. Westport, Conn.: Greenwood, 1977.

Halberstam, D., *The Best and the Brightest*. New York: Fawcett, 1973.

Hoffman, B. and Dukas, H., *Albert Einstein: Creator and Rebel*. New York: Viking Press, 1972.

Keller, H., *The Story of My Life*. Garden City, N.Y.: Doubleday, 1954.

Kurland, G., *Benjamin Franklin: America's Universal Man*. Charlotteville, N.Y.: Sam Harwood Press, 1972.

Lewis, D. L., *King: A Biography*. Second edition. Urbana, Illinois: University of Illinois Press, 1978.

Orga, A., *Beethoven: His Life and Times*. New York: Two Continents Press, 1978.

Index

Abstract ideas, 13
Accelerated programs, 67–69
Achievement tests, 56
American Shakespeare Theatre Center, 79
Astor Program, 66
Avon, Conn., 66

Baldwin-Identification Matrix (BIM), 76
Baltimore, Md., 67–68
Bates, Joseph, 67–68
Beethoven, Ludwig van, 21
Behavior-rating scales, 59
Bernal, E., 76
Bible, 23
Biographical inventory, 59, 75
Bloom, Benjamin S., 40
Boredom, 47–48
Brainstorming, 78
Bronx High School of Science, 66
Buck, Pearl S., 33

California, University of, 68
California Tests of Mental Maturity, 26, 27–28
Carter, Jimmy, 31
Cervantes, Miguel de, 24
Charlemagne, 24
China, 23
Clench, William, 36
Cleveland, Ohio, 65–66
Cohan, George M., 35
Collecting, 18, 36
Columbus, Christopher, 24
Concentration, 10
Constantinople, 25
Copernicus, 24
Cornell University, 68
Court of the Eight Colleges, 25
Cox, Catherine, 29
Cradles of Eminence (Goertzel), 17, 37
Creativity, 18–19, 31, 41, 76
  and madness, 23
  testing, 57–59

Creativity and Intelligence (Getzels & Jackson), 57–58
Curiosity, 10

da Vinci, Leonardo, 24
Daydreaming, 36
Difference, sense of, 45–46
Disadvantaged gifted children, 72–79
Discrimination. *See* Disadvantaged gifted children; Sexism
Downs, Cornelia, 34

Edison, Thomas Alva, 18, 19, 48
Education. *See* Schools and education
Einstein, Albert, 10, 11, 12, 41, 48
Enrichment programs, 69–70
Erasmus, 24

Family. *See* Home and family; Parents
Fantasies, 36
Franklin, Benjamin, 10

Galileo Galilei, 24
George Washington University, 70
Gershwin, George and Ira, 34
Getzels, J. W., 57–58
Gifted and Talented Act, 31–32
Goertzel, Victor and Mildred, 17, 37
Governor's School (Salem, N.C.), 66
Guilford, J. P., 30

Heinecken, Christian, 13–15
Hobbies, 35–36
Hollingsworth, Leta, 29
Home and family, 33–38. *See also* Parents
Horizons Unlimited, 66
Houston, Tex., 76

Individualized Education Programs (IEPs), 70–71
Insanity, 23
Insight, 10–11
Intelligence quotient (IQ), 7, 26, 29, 30, 31, 53–56, 74
Isolation, 50–51

Jackson, P. W., 57–58
Javits, Jacob, 31
Jefferson, Thomas, 25
Johns Hopkins University, 67–68

Keene, N. H., 66
Kendall, Edward C., 36
King, Martin Luther, 33
Kotschenreuther, Michael, 68

Leonardo da Vinci, 24
Luther, Martin, 24

Maazel, Lorin, 15, 16
Madness, 23
Magellan, Ferdinand, 24
Marland, Sidney, 3, 71, 74–75
Medicine men, 23
Memory, 13
Mentor programs, 69–70
Mexican-Americans, 76
Michelangelo, 24
Middle Ages, 24
Milton, John, 17
Minnesota, 68
Mohammed the Conqueror, 25
Motivation, lack of, 73

National Defense Education Act, 30
New Haven, Conn., 78–79
New York City, 55–56, 66
New York University, 29
Noncomformity, 48–49

Office of the Gifted and Talented, 31

Parents, 61–62, 76. *See also* Home and family
Pascal, Blaise, 17
Peer nomination, 62, 75
Peterson, Roger T., 18
Petrarch, 24
Physical development, 9
Picasso, Pablo, 48, 49
Plato, 24, 25
Prejudice, 42
Princeton University, 68
Problems of the gifted, 45–52
    and disadvantaged, 73–75
Programs for the gifted, 64–71
    and disadvantaged, 76–79
Progressive Education, 29

Rachmaninoff, Sergei, 48
Raphael, 24
Reading and books, 10, 35
Renaissance, the, 24–25
Republic, The (Plato), 24, 25
Rockford, Ill., 61–62
Russians, 30

St. Louis, Mo., 25–26
Salem, N.C., 66
Schools and education, 3, 13, 24, 25–32, 34, 40–44. *See also* Programs for the gifted
Self-concept. *See* Home and family; Parents; Schools and education
Self-contained classes, 65–67

Sexism, 42, 51–52
Shakespeare, William, 24
Sidis, William James, 26
Sitting up, early, 9
Soviet Union, 30
Sputnik, 30
Stanford-Benet Intelligence Scale, 26
Stanford University, 29
Stern, Isaac, 33
Stimulation, lack of, 73

Talcott Mountain Science Program, 66
Talking, early, 10
Teachers, 39–44, 60–61, 75
Terman, Lewis, 15, 29
Testing, 7, 23, 53–63, 75–76
Thinking, 40
Torrance, E. Paul, 30, 51, 52, 58, 76
Torrance Tests of Creative Thinking, 58, 75
Toys, 35
Transformations, 79
Travel, 36
Tribal leaders, 23
Turkey, 25

Walking, early, 9
Wechsler Intelligence Scale for Children (WISC), 26

Zorbaugh, Harvey, 29

About the Author

Gilda Berger, a former teacher of exceptional children in the New York City, Long Beach, and Great Neck school systems and currently a member of the Council for Exceptional Children, is the author of seven books, including *Learning Disabilities and Handicaps* (an Impact Book) and *Physical Disabilities,* both for Franklin Watts.

Gilda, the mother of two teenage daughters and the wife of author Melvin Berger, lives with her family in Great Neck and is currently at work on her next book for Franklin Watts on the subject of speech disabilities.

WITHDRAWN